He never stopped loving you

Finding comfort in God's everlasting love

Jeanette Stohlmann

He never stopped loving you
Finding comfort in God's everlasting love

For my dear sisters:

Mary Lou, Ruth Ann, and Marcella,

as we look forward to seeing our brother

in heaven.

Preface

What happens when life throws us a curve? When

everything is going great and then...tragedy strikes. We may get

angry. We may cry. Or we may try to cover up our true feelings.

How does experiencing tragedy affect our relationship

with God? Does it change our attitude to God? Do we feel He

doesn't love us as much as before? Do we feel He **stopped** loving

us?

But the truth is **He never stopped loving us**! God has a

whole different way of looking at things. He sees the whole

picture of events in the lives of people all around the world.

While we focus on our little worlds, God sees everything and

views it in the context of the eternal welfare of each person.

In His love, He wants everyone to be saved!

2 Peter 3:9

"The Lord is not slow in keeping his promise, as some understand
slowness. He is patient with you, **not wanting anyone to perish,**
but everyone to come to repentance."

When it seems like our world is crashing around us and

caving in on us, **God is still in control**. Believe it or not, God

knows what each of us is going through!

God is in control. **No matter how bad things get, we know how the story ends**...with Jesus' glorious return on the last day and every knee bowing to Jesus! Therefore we can be still and know that He is God.

Psalm 46

"God is our refuge and strength,
a very present help in trouble.
Therefore we will not fear though the earth gives way, though the mountains be moved into the heart of the sea,
though its waters roar and foam,
though the mountains tremble at its swelling.
> There is a river whose streams make glad the city of God,
> the holy habitation of the Most High.
> God is in the midst of her, she shall not be moved,
> God will help her when morning dawns.
> The nations rage, the kingdoms totter,
> he utters his voice, the earth melts.
Come behold the works of the LORD,
how he has brought desolations on the earth.
He makes wars cease to the end of the earth;
he breaks the bow and shatters the spear,
he burns the chariots with fire.
'Be still and know that I am God.
I will be exalted among the nations, I will be exalted in the earth!' "

May God comfort you with His everlasting love!

Jeanette Dorothy Stohlmann   January 2012

Chapters

Chapter 1   Rabbit trails

My three sisters and I doted on our younger brother, Ed, the baby of the family. And yet, we all looked up to him, too. He was the entrepreneur of the family with his farm seed business and large dairy, and the hardest worker I have ever known. He also found time to invent things, lead in the local government, and make evangelism calls. He was strong and healthy and that is why we never expected what would happen.

Mayo Clinic trips

For years he had gone to the Mayo Clinic in Rochester, once a year for a health screening, including liver check. This was because he had a rare occurrence of eye cancer, and even though the cancer was arrested in the eye, there was a chance it could metastasize or spread to the liver. Year after year, he received a clean bill of liver health, until he was 47 years old. The cancer had spread to the liver. He was given 3 months to live, but due to experimental treatment, and by the grace of God, he lived to be 52. After a valiant fight with his illness, he passed away on August 30, 2006.

The problem with rabbit trails

In my anger at what happened, my trust in God wavered. I followed some rabbit trails of doubt and lack of trust. Pastor Richard Eyer, in his book, <u>Pastoral Care Under the Cross</u>, says: "We think we know how the future should unfold and who should be able to live to a ripe old age. And when people die too soon, we think we cannot trust God. Maybe He forgot to 'mind the store.' " *

*Eyer, Richard C. <u>Pastoral Care Under the Cross</u>. © 1994, Concordia Publishing House, St. Louis, MO.

The problem with rabbit trails is that they bring no satisfaction and lead away from God, instead of to God who is the only source of true comfort. But God never gave up on me or let go of me. I could relate to the lyrics of the contemporary Christian song, "You Never Let Go", by Matt Redman.*

* www.Christian-lyrics.net/matt-redman/you-never-let-go-lyrics.html

Stages of Grief

Grieving is a process that takes time. Elizabeth Kubler-Ross developed the now-famous five stages of grief. They are: 1. Denial; 2. Anger; 3. Bargaining; 4. Depression; 5.Acceptance. The final step is the acceptance of the death of a loved one. *

*Elizabeth Kubler-Ross grief.com/the-five-stages-of-grief/

Why so soon?

It is always **too early** for a loved one to die. In the early stages of my grief, I had a hard time understanding why this happened. Why so young? Why now? How could I trust in God like before? Look at what He did to my brother.

"Look at what He did to my brother," I told a kind minister.

"Yes, look at what He did to your brother," the minister replied. "He gave Him eternal life in the kingdom of heaven."

The sad, earthly view

Grieving for the loss of my dear brother, I was only looking at things from my sad, earthly point of view. I could no longer visit and talk with my brother. I could no longer go to his farmhouse where I grew up and stay overnight and enjoy the pleasant childhood memories that gathered there.

And death was just an ugly mark on the happy timeline of his life. It was way too soon and it was against nature. The younger ones are not supposed to die before the older ones. But all this was **my** view of life and the way things should be.

God's bird's eye view

God sees things differently. By welcoming my brother home, God spared my brother many years of work and trials on this earth. God took him to be in heaven, with Him, to experience the joy and peace of eternity.

My brother never married but he had accomplished many things in his short life. He actively supported worldwide missions and was a devout Christian. **Maybe God just figured that his work was done on this earth.** Maybe there was someone who attended the funeral who heard the Gospel message for the first time. Maybe, it was just his time to go.

God has a time set

My brother, Ed, had mentioned a month or so before he died that God has set a time for each of us to die. He also mentioned that he really wanted to live, but if God called him home, that was O.K. too!

It was just his time... God knows best.

~ ~

Psalm 31:14-16

"But I trust in you, O LORD;
I say, 'You are my God.'
My times are in your hands;
deliver me from my enemies and
from those who pursue me.
Let your face shine on your servant;
save me in your unfailing love."

Isaiah 55:9
"As the heavens are higher than the earth, **so are my ways higher than your ways and my thoughts than your thoughts.**"
✴ ✴

Acceptance

About two years after my brother died, I penned this poem. It shows my gradual acceptance of the will of God and trust in the loving wisdom of God.

If
by Jeanette Stohlmann 2008

If I could spend a day in heaven
And hear God's holy voice
And see the face of Jesus
I always would rejoice.

If I could touch an angel
And see the saints around
Then I would never worry
And never wear a frown
If I could hug my brother
Who died at a young age
I would throw away my anger
And let go of my rage.

If I could hear heaven's music
And everyone in tune.
I would never more complain
That people die too soon.

If I could feel the love of Jesus
Shining all around
My eyes would melt to tears
I wouldn't make a sound.

If I could spend a day in heaven
And rest upon a cloud
Then I would tell the world
'I love you,' right out loud!

Certainty of eternal life

Now five years have passed since my brother died. I have

read the book <u>90 Minutes in Heaven</u> by Don Piper, which

really helped me to realize that I would not wish my

brother back to this earth after he had experienced the

joys of heaven! God's promise of eternal life is certain and

sure. Those who believe in Jesus are in the very presence

of God!

+ + + + + + + + + + + + + + + + + +

John 10:27-28

"My sheep listen to my voice; I know them, and they follow me. **I give them eternal life,** and they shall never perish; **no one can snatch them out of my hand.**"

Titus 1:1-2

Titus 1:1-2
"Paul, a servant of God and an apostle of Jesus Christ for the faith of God's elect and the knowledge of the truth that leads to godliness--a faith and knowledge resting on **the hope of eternal life,** which **God, who does not lie,** promised before the **beginning of time..."**

~ ~ ~ ~ ~ ~ ~ ~ ~ ~ ~ ~ ~ ~ ~ ~

No gaps in Jesus' love

Jesus' words assure us of this in Matthew 28:20: **"And surely I am with you always, to the very end of the age."**

All who are left on earth, sorrowing and grieving the death of a loved one can take comfort in this passage, knowing that Jesus' love remains the same.

Hebrews 13:8
"Jesus Christ is the same yesterday and today and forever."

Keeping our eyes fixed on Jesus

Many trials, temptations, doubts, etc. try to distract us from

fixing our eyes on Jesus. **But it is Jesus alone whom we will**

see when we die, at the end of the long tunnel of light.

Therefore, **if we trust in Him and His Word, we will be**

ushered into eternal life, as He promised.

~~~~~~

Hebrews 12:2

"**Let us fix our eyes on Jesus**, the author and perfecter of our
faith, who for the joy set before him endured the cross,
scorning its shame, and sat down on the right hand of the throne
of God."

~~~~~~

Nothing can separate us from the love of God. Life can't.

Death can't. The devil and the powers of hell can't. Doubts can't.

Trouble can't. Persecution can't. Things that happened in the

past can't. Sin can't. Things happening now can't. Things that will

happen in the future can't.

Romans 8:38,39

"For I am convinced that **neither death nor life, neither angels nor demons, neither the present nor the future, nor any powers, neither height nor depth, nor anything else in all creation, will be able to separate us from the love of God that is in Christ Jesus, our Lord.**"

~ ~

Chapter 2
Teacher, I can't sleep at night

Sometimes, even though we may have our own inner turmoil going on, God still calls on us to think of others. That's what happened when I was still grieving over my brother and teaching in a middle school. My U.S. History students were required to write an essay on what they were "running away from", a take-off on our study of the runaway slaves in the Civil War.

Many interesting essays were written. One student was trying to escape bad dreams from fleeing war-torn Ethiopia. One student was running from an eating disorder, etc. But the essay that caught my eye was the sleep disorder one.

" **I can't sleep at night**. I am afraid of dying. "

My student was a healthy eighth-grader, but his problem had to do with spiritual matters. He was afraid of death be-cause of the impending wrath of God. But Jesus came to earth to free us from the fear of death.

~~ ~~ ~~ ~~ ~~ ~~ ~~ ~~ ~~ ~~ ~~ ~~ ~~ ~~ ~~ ~~ ~~ ~~ ~~ ~~
Hebrews 2:14-15
"Since the children have flesh and blood, he [Jesus] too shared in their humanity so that by his death he might destroy him who holds the power of death--that is, the devil-- **and free those who all their lives were held in slavery by their fear of death.**"

Jesus frees us from fear of death

Jesus frees us from the fear of death, but my student had never been introduced to Jesus. His family was not Christian. So, when all of the other students left for the day, I asked him privately about his essay. He explained that he would stay up as late as possible, without sleeping, because he was afraid to die. That same week, one of his Christian friends handed him a free Bible.

A year later, he came to me when no other students were in the classroom.

"Hello!" he smiled. "I'm not afraid to go to sleep anymore."

He looked peaceful and very happy and told me that he now knew Jesus.

John 3:16
For God so loved the world that he gave his one and only Son, that whoever believes in him shall not perish, but have eternal life."

Casting our cares on God

Christians sometimes have trouble sleeping at night for many reasons. We may be anxious about problems of this life, or wrestling with doubts or dealing with pains and fears for the future. But we can cast all our cares on God, for He cares for us.

I Peter 5:7
"Cast all your anxiety on him because he cares for you."

Did you note the word "**all**"? "Cast **all** your anxiety on him because he cares for you." Do not hold anything back. Cast all your anxiety on Him. Cast your worries, fears, and your burdens on God.

Try this experiment.

1. **Think about what your burden is right now.**

2. **Give it to God.** Matthew 19:26 "...with God all things are possible."

3. **Forget about it.**

4. **Trust in God's unfailing love.**

   How do you feel? Relieved? Hopeful? Confident? God rescued us from our fears and He rescued us from death and the devil. He wants us to have joy now and continuing forever!

God can do abundantly more than we can ask or think. When we place our burden in God's hands, **we trust His power, His enduring love for us, and His impeccable timing**. In faith we can bring our problem to God, just by talking to God. For example:

"**Dear God,**
 It's me. You know the burden that I have been carrying. I am tired of carrying it, so I am going to give it to You. I know that with You all things are possible. I can trust in Your unfailing love. Please take my burden and give me peace.
In Jesus' name. Amen

No request is too small for God

All requests, whether small or great, can be laid before God's throne of grace. Sometimes it is easy to forget that we are King's kids. We don't have to fret over problems. We can take them immediately to the Lord, the King of Kings in prayer.

One time I was looking for something in the house that I had mislaid. After a frustrating search, I remembered that God knows all things and he knows our every need, big or small. After I prayed, I easily found the lost item and praised God!

Perseverance in prayer

What about the times people pray for years and there seems to be no answer? A woman prayed for her husband to know the Lord for more than 50 years. Finally, on his deathbed, her husband confessed faith in Jesus, his Lord!

Why does God sometimes require us to wait for an answer?... Is God teaching us to be persistent and patient? Is God developing character in us so we can make it through the long haul?

~ ~

Romans 5:2-5

"...And we rejoice in the hope of the glory of God. Not only so, but we also rejoice in our sufferings, because we know that **suffering produces perseverance; perseverance, character; and character, hope.** And hope does not disappoint us, because God has poured out his love into our hearts by the Holy Spirit, whom he has given us."

God gives rest to the weary

When we give our burdens to Jesus, resting in His unfailing love, we can sleep in peace as Jesus promised us:

Matthew 11:28

"Come to me, all you who are weary and burdened, and I will give you rest."

Chapter 3 The importance of cards

Even in the age of e-cards, I still like receiving cards in

the mail. I love the colors, and I like to display and reread the

cards I receive. When I had pneumonia last year, I received nice

"get well" cards, but the one I treasured was from a friend from

the women's guild at church. It had a picture of a little girl

praying and the Bible verse from **I Peter 5:7 "Cast all your**

anxiety on him because he cares for you."

People need reassurance

When people are sick or recovering from a car accident or grieving over the loss of a loved one, **they need reassurance that God still loves them.** Of course, they can read the many promises of God in the Bible... **But it is especially heart-warming when another person reaches out to them in sympathy and love!**

That's why sending cards is so important! When storms of life hit hard, they can buffet a fragile faith. That's why **people need encouragement** during tough times! Christians can **listen to the Holy Spirit** telling them to befriend people in their tough times. It is so vital that we build up and encourage one another in the faith!

~ ~

Galatians 6:10
"Therefore, as we have opportunity, **let us do good to all people, especially to those who belong to the family of believers.**"

28

Dr. Ron Ostten, a pastor from Louisiana, gave a sermon shortly after his oldest daughter, Sandra, was killed when the vehicle she was driving stalled on a railroad crossing and was hit by an oncoming train. He describes how his family was so grateful for cards and notes sent: "Many people have sent us literature and notes to encourage us; this has been a great encouragement. Don't count it lightly concerning the notes you send to a grieving family or person. The notes, cards, phone calls, and email have been a great comfort in many ways."

*blessedquietness.com/journal/housechu/letgo.htm

----

2 Corinthians 1:3-4

"Praise be to the God and Father of our Lord Jesus Christ, the Father of compassion and the God of all comfort, who comforts us in all our troubles, so that we can comfort those in any trouble with the comfort we ourselves have received from God."

God loves people through us

Through the power of God working in us, we can **do good**! Yes! Send cards! Visit the sick! Feed the hungry! Comfort the dying. **God communicates His love through us**!

~ ~

Ephesians 2:10
"For we are God's workmanship, created in Christ Jesus to do good works, which God prepared in advance for us to do."

I used my many years of painting with acrylics to brighten the walls of a local Veteran's Home. One veteran who received my painting for his room commented on how delighted he was to wake up to the beautiful painting every morning!

Sewing quilts for Gillette Hospital patients also keeps me busy. When the parents see these colorful quilts, they are overwhelmed by the kindness of strangers who would make such a loving gift for their sick child!

A miracle quilt story

Of the many people I have sewn quilts for, I will always remember the older woman I met who suffered from **nightmares** and depression. She had seen my quilts and wanted one of her own. She wanted it designed a certain way with her favorite cartoon character. As with my other quilts, I agreed to make the quilt for free, as God freely gives His grace to us. I presented it to her with a letter describing the love of Jesus. And then a miracle of God happened! She later told me that since she started using that handmade quilt on her bed, the nightmares went away! Praise God!

Good works are fruits of faith

All this "doing good" is not burdensome. It is joy! It is a natural fruit of our faith.

Galatians 5:22

"But the **fruit of the Spirit is love**, joy, peace, patience, kindness, goodness, faithfulness..."

+

I John 4:19
"We love because he **first** loved us."

+

Feeding the hungry

An inspiring story appeared on YouTube about a grandmother who had a desire to feed the needy children who go hungry in the summer months because they no longer have access to the school's free and reduced lunches. Eileen R. serves noon meals to over 500 Omaha children a day at the Holy Name Church cafeteria. The program is funded by the U.S. Department of Agriculture and the Heartland Food Bank. The meals are provided free to any child who comes. And they can get a bonus---a cookie and a hug from Eileen! *

*http:/www.youtube.com/watch?v=Sck4lTxtHl

Music to comfort a suffering person

Perhaps God will use a song you sing to a suffering person to call that person back to him. The meaningful and powerful hymn, "What God Ordains is Always Good" was first published in 1674. It assures us that God will provide comfort after we have gone through suffering.*

The words of the hymn "What God Ordains is Always Good" were written by a German teacher, Samuel Rodigast, to encourage a sick friend, and the hymn has encouraged Christians, in their suffering, ever since. Not only does the hymn proclaim an acceptance of whatever happens in life, but it also announces that God is right there to help us in the midst of our suffering.*

* http://religiousaffections.org/featured/samuel-rodigast-whatever-god/

What God ordains is always good;
His will abideth holy.
As He directs my life for me,
I follow meek and lowly.
My God indeed
In every need
Doth well know how to shield me;
To Him, then I will yield me.

What God ordains is always good.
This loving thought attends me.
No poison can be in the cup
That my Physician sends me.
My God is true.
Each morn anew
I'll trust His grace unending,
My life to Him commending.

What God ordains is always good.
He is my Friend and Father;
He suffers naught to do me harm,
Tho' many storms may gather.
Now I may know
Both joy and woe,
Some day I shall see clearly
That He hath loved me dearly.

What God ordains is always good.
Though I the cup am drinking
Which savors now of bitterness,
I take it without shrinking.

For after grief
God grants relief,
My heart with comfort filling
And all my sorrow stilling.

What God ordains is always
good.
This truth remains unshaken.
Though sorrow, need, or death
be mine,
I shall not be forsaken.
I fear no harm,
For with His arm
He shall embrace and shield me;
So to my God I yield me

*The Lutheran Hymnal. #521 Words by Samuel Rodigast.

I Peter 5:10

"And the God of all grace, who called you to his eternal glory in Christ, **after you have suffered a little while**, will himself restore you and make you strong, firm and steadfast."

Chapter 4 Why do bad things happen?

Tough question... We live in a **sin-sick world**. Whether it is

our sins that cause something or the sins of people in the world

that cause something bad to happen, sin definitely is a problem.

When people **fail to take care of their health**, they may get

sick. That is a natural consequence. But also, the way **people get**

old and die, is the direct result

of sin. **"For the wages of sin is**

death..." Romans 6:23

Why daily suffering?

But what about suffering

which goes on day after day,

where death is not the sweet

release to glory? God always has a reason for allowing this

suffering. Maybe it is to make us **empathetic** to the suffering of

others with similar sicknesses. Maybe our suffering **increases**

our reliance on God. Maybe **our endurance of our suffering**

encourages others in their faith. **Maybe God wants to display**

His power in healing our suffering or helping us to endure.

Maybe God wants to change bad things into good! Only our

great God can do this...change evil into good.

Joseph's life changes from bad to good!

In the Bible, Joseph had been sold into slavery by his own

brothers in Canaan. Years later, after other unfortunate

incidents, including being jailed unjustly, Joseph was elevated to

a position of leadership in which he was able to save God's people

from famine in Egypt.

In Nancy Guthrie's book, Be Still My Soul: Embracing God's

Purpose and Provision in Suffering, the author explains short

term suffering and long term blessing: "If we look at the

disasters that befell Joseph in the Old Testament, we see that

what seemed tragic in the short term was actually a blessing in

the long term." *

*Guthrie, Nancy. Be Still My Soul: Embracing God's Purpose and Provision in Suffering.
Crossway Books, Wheaton, IL © 2010.

Genesis 50:19-21

"But Joseph said to them, 'Don't be

afraid...You intended to harm me, but

God intended it for good to accomplish

what is now being done, the saving of

many lives. So then, don't be afraid. I

will provide for you and your children.'

And he reassured them and spoke kindly

to them."

Why Memory Loss?

My mother, a wonderfully devout Christian, lived to be 90 years old; but unfortunately, the last ten years of her life, her mind was clouded with memory loss. Towards the end of her life, she no longer said my name. The last time I visited her, she flashed me a beautiful smile which told me that she knew who I was. I will always treasure that smile!

With my mom, it was so clear how God used her suffering as a witness, even in her years of weakness. She loved to sing and even when she didn't know what day it was anymore, she still sang all the words to hymns from her memory. It was so **comforting to know that God preserves faith in His children,** even in their weakness. One of the hymns she sang was "My Hope is Built on Nothing Less" *

My hope is built on nothing less
Than Jesus' blood and righteousness;
I dare not trust the sweetest frame,
But wholly lean on Jesus' name.
On Christ, the solid Rock, I stand;
All other ground is sinking sand.

When darkness veils His lovely face,
I rest on His unchanging grace;
In every high and stormy gale
My anchor holds within the veil.
On Christ, the solid Rock, I stand;
All other ground is sinking sand.
*The Lutheran Hymnal #370

God's faithfulness is displayed

My mom sang, "When darkness veils His lovely face, I trust in His unchanging grace..." There she was...in a wheelchair, her mind all foggy...lonely (My dad had passed away after they had been married for over 50 years)...There she was...a mere shadow of her former vivacious self...Yes, darkness had veiled Jesus' lovely face, temporarily because of her earthly suffering, **but with the eyes of faith, she could still see Jesus**! She could still trust in His unchanging grace, not by her own power, but by the power of the Holy Spirit, working in her heart since her baptism day, 90 years before! But there was another reason my mother was allowed to suffer with memory loss...

A witness for Jesus

My mother had home health aides attending her at home, and insisted that after supper, they would read the Bible and a devotional book to her. No doubt, these workers were also nourished by the Word! Also, my mother insisted on going to church, with the assistance, of course, of her home health aides. Through this weekly practice, the aides also grew in their faith. One young woman started attending church regularly and even sent her young daughter to a Christian school! And so God used my mother, even in her weakness, to strengthen others in the holy faith!

Joni's faith: a witness for the world

Joni Eareckson Tada, internationally known writer and artist, suffered the tragedy of paralysis from a swimming pool diving accident. In spite of the many inconveniences which her disability has caused, she still wholeheartedly claims Romans 8:28 as one of her favorite Bible verses. She is pictured below sketching.

Romans 8:28

"And we know that in all things God works for the good of those who love him, who have been called according to his purpose."

~ ~

Joni has persevered and even **learned to paint** while holding a brush in her mouth. The way in which God turned a terrible accident into a **wonderful witness for the world** is truly awesome! *

*Eareckson Tada, Joni. Ordinary People, Extraordinary Faith, copyright © 2001 by Joni Eareckson Tada, printed in U.S.A.

God displays His power

Remember the story of Jesus healing the man born blind? The disciples wondered why the man was born blind. They wondered if it was because the man or his parents had sinned. In John 9:3 we read Jesus' response:

"Neither this man nor his parents sinned," said Jesus, " **but this happened so that the work of God might be displayed in his life.**"

When Jesus healed the blind man and restored his sight, the man could not resist telling everyone. **Sometimes God miraculously heals people** whom doctors have written off as hopelessly ill. Their stories of healing are shared, and in this way, **God is glorified** for being the Lord of life!

God's power displayed in our weakness

In <u>Pastoral Care Under the Cross</u>*, Pastor Richard Eyer, says that when we kneel at the foot of the cross, we can clearly see our loving Savior suffering in our place, dying our death. Jesus comes to us in our own suffering and assures us," **My grace is sufficient for you, for my power is made perfect in weakness.**" 2 Corinthians 12:9

*Eyer, Richard C. <u>Pastoral Care Under the Cross</u>, © 1994. Concordia Publishing House, St. Louis, Missouri.

Something beautiful out of the ashes

What if, out of the suffering...out of the ashes...something beautiful emerges? Like an inspirational book? Like a story of encouragement told to strangers? Like a song written for church? Like a stronger faith? Like a peace, so deep? Like the salvation of many souls?

Maybe the fiery testing we endure and the spiritual deserts that we wander through, are the starting place for something so marvelous, that when it happens, we know it must be the Lord's doing! And maybe that marvelous thing will lead someone to Jesus!

Horatio Spafford's suffering led to a beautiful hymn

The following is the true story of the composer of the famous hymn, "It is Well with My Soul". Horatio Spafford suffered almost unimaginable personal tragedy. Nevertheless, **out of his immense suffering, came forth one of the most beautiful hymns ever written.**

Horatio Spafford was a Chicago lawyer. He and his wife, Anna, were close friends of the famous preacher, D.L. Moody. In 1870, the **Spafford's only son died of scarlet fever at the age of four.** In 1871, all of Horatio's real estate holdings on the shores of Lake Michigan were destroyed by the great **Chicago Fire.**

In 1873 the Spaffords planned to join D. L. Moody, traveling around Great Britain on a huge evangelism campaign. When Horatio's wife and four daughters got on a steamer heading for Europe, Horatio stayed behind a while to finish a business deal in Chicago.

Sadly, nine days later, Horatio received a telegram from Anna, his wife, that said, "Saved alone." **The steamer carrying his wife and four daughters had collided with an English vessel.** The steamer sank in twelve minutes, taking the lives of the four daughters!

When Horatio heard the chilling news, he boarded the next ship out of New York to join his bereaved wife. After the ship passed by the three-mile deep place in the ocean where his daughters drowned, Horatio went to his cabin on the ship and wrote these hymn lyrics:

It is Well with My Soul *   Horatio Spafford

When peace like a river, attendeth my way,
When sorrows like sea billows roll;
Whatever my lot, Thou has taught me to say,
It is well, it is well, with my soul.

Though Satan should buffet, though trials should come,
Let this blest assurance control,
That Christ has regarded my helpless estate,
And hath shed His own blood for my soul.

*   www.biblestudycharts.com

~~~~~~

Suffering -- God's megaphone

It is well-worth the effort to rent the movie, "Shadowlands",*
the story of C.S. Lewis' marriage. The tear-jerking movie, which
also was a play, tells of C. S. Lewis' own struggles with suffering
as he experiences the sickness and death of his young wife.
Before this tragedy strikes in his own life, C.S. Lewis explains to
his fellow theologians that suffering is God's trumpet call on the
world.

C.S. Lewis compares pain to a **"megaphone to rouse a deaf
world"**.* When things are going smoothly and people are well-
fed and content, this world seems like a fine place to stay.
Suffering nudges people to look up to God for help, in a fallen
world where death and danger wait at every turn.

* Price Entertainment (1993). <u>Shadowlands.</u>
  *<u>www.imdb.com/title/tt0108101/**quotes**</u>

Victory after suffering

In John 11, Jesus comforted Martha at the grave of her dead brother, Lazarus, and then performed the awesome miracle of raising her brother to life. In John 11:25 Jesus said, "... **I am the resurrection and the life. He who believes in me will live, even though he dies...**"

Death is but a gateway into eternal life. Jesus, through His hours of patient suffering, has made it possible for us to be immediately swept into glory, at our death. As we kneel at the cross, we **remember the Easter victory that followed Jesus' suffering.** We know that if we endure suffering in this life, **there is victory in the end.** *

*Eyer, Richard C., <u>Pastoral Care Under the Cross</u>, © 1994, Concordia Publishing House, St. Louis, Missouri.

Chapter 5 Something better for you!

A baby surprise

A young married woman, after ten years of mothering her three young children, with all their shenanigans, had finally reached a point where she could return to her career! And then she found out she was expecting a fourth child.

At first she was disappointed and said, "I again had to put all that I wanted on the back burner and try to figure out how I could fit this little new person into a life that I felt was already full."

In time, the mother accepted it as the will of God. After the child was born, she rejoiced! Now, her joy has increased exponentially and she could not imagine life without her fourth addition!

The mother said, "Interestingly enough this child was named Gracie, taken from the feeling I found in my heart to be thankful and gracious for the beautiful gift... Unexpected or not, my life would not be the same without her." *

* http://www.professorhouse.com/Family/Pregnancy/Articles/An-Unexpected-Pregnancy/

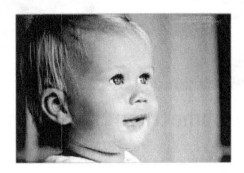

A better location

Downsizing is not an anomaly in these days of economic uncertainty. About ten years ago I was teaching ESL [English as a Second Language] at a middle school. I loved teaching there and it was my fourth year when downsizing hit. My school needed less ESL teachers so I was reassigned to another middle school. I remember my trepidation, thinking that I did not know anyone at the new school. But...as God planned it, I loved the new school even more than the old school. The new middle school had windows in the classrooms, where the other school did not. Also, there was better ventilation, a bigger classroom, a theater for plays, and friendly people, too.

Total healing

A young wife prayed for her husband to be cured of cancer. But, as time passed, her husband's condition worsened, and he passed away.

"If only I had prayed harder," she thought. "Then he would have lived."

Sometimes, on this earth, when we ask God for healing, He graciously grants it. Miraculously, the pain, the sickness, the cancer is gone! And the power of God is displayed and God is praised! But sometimes, on this earth, when we ask God for healing, He most graciously says................"I have something better for your loved one: Perfect healing and perfect peace forever!" And God is certainly praised for giving the gift of eternal life!

From heartache to happily married

A woman shared a story on the web, entitled "God the Matchmaker or How I Met My Husband". While she had been saddened by a college break-up, she admits the break-up was a good thing because **God had a better man in mind for her to marry.**

Now after 30 years of marriage to this "better guy" she says," I am more in love with Mark today than I was the day we married. He is my best friend on earth and he is truly my soul mate--**all arranged by God. God the Holy Matchmaker...How COOL is that? The Lord intervened and made the path, broken along the way--but it led directly to my heart's desire even before I knew...**" *

* http://cjv123.hubpages.com/hub/God-the-Matchmaker-or-How-I-Met-My-Husband-Ending

A happy reunion

When a loved one dies, we can be certain that he/she we will be reunited with all of our sainted loved ones in heaven. And if we die, we can be certain that God has something infinitely better waiting for us in heaven.

I Corinthians 2:9

"No eye has seen, no ear has heard, no mind has conceived what God has prepared for those who love him."

The joy of God walking with us

We can delight in the companionship of God as He walks with us through the grief, trials, and tribulations of this life. Even in old age, He will still sustain us. In His time, God will call us home. But as long as God gives us life on this earth, He has a purpose for us...which may include the job of praying for others.

Isaiah 46:4

"Even to your old age and gray hairs I am he, I am he who will sustain you. I have made you and I will carry you; I will sustain you and I will rescue you."

54

Life is hard
anonymous author

Life is hard
But don't let its hardness
Turn you hard as stone.
Remember God loves you
And you never walk alone.

Arlena prays for others

Arlena G., age 44, shared her story of triumph over pain, while feeling "trapped in a 100-year-old body that is nothing but pain 24 hours a day..."

She continued, "I have had two lower back surgeries with fusions, three neck surgeries with fusions... I live with severe headaches and my body is so filled with pain...But I pray... because that's about all I can do... Each and everyone of you will be in my daily prayers and may God bless you and help you with your pain."

www.ourhopeonline.com/id7.html

55

Chapter 6 Trusting God

Proverbs 3:5
"Trust in the LORD with all your heart
and lean not on your own understanding..."

Linda's story

In 2009 Linda was in tears and tormented by anxiety and depression. Linda, a married woman with a family, remembered having anxiety even as a child. Finally she found a Christian mentor who walked her through Bible passages of comfort and trust. She especially liked Timothy 1:7 and said, "When I found this scripture, I stood on it with everything in me. Every time I would start to feel panicky, I would quote this scripture."

2 Timothy 1:7
"For God did not give us a spirit of timidity, but a spirit of power, of love and of self-discipline."

She continued to pray and ask God for his strength and help. She was healed of her anxiety and gave this testimony: "I renewed my mind with God's Word, and became victorious." *

*   www.testimonyshare.com/god-healed-me-from-anxiety-and-depressi...

Resting in God

Isaiah 30:15

"This is what the Sovereign LORD, the Holy One of Israel, says: 'In repentance and **rest** is your salvation, in **quietness and trust** is your strength...' "

+

We can safely trust God to help us because He loves us and cares for us. At the same time, He is holy so He can do no wrong. He is changeless so His love endures forever. Great is the Lord. He is holy and just. By His power we trust in His love!

God is: 1. **Loving and sympathetic**
            2. **Caring**
               3. **Holy**
                  4. **Changeless**

1. God is loving and sympathetic

Lack of consistent love can confuse us and hurtful words can sting just like an arrow to the heart. Where can one find a never-ending fountain of love and acceptance? **It is only from God.** Only Jesus knows every hurt, every pain, every unkind word that has stabbed us in the heart, every feeling of rejection, every grief. **Resting in Jesus we know that we are totally and completely loved now and forever!**

Isaiah 53:4

"Surely he took up our infirmities and **carried our sorrows...**"

Psalm 56:8

"Record my lament; **list my tears on your scroll-- are they not in your record?**"

Remember the Bible story of Jesus mourning at the grave of his friend, Lazarus, who had died? **"Jesus wept."** This verse in John 11:35, is the shortest verse in the Bible, and yet it shows the compassion of God! Jesus sympathizes with us through all of our sadness.

And God is loving. In I John 4:8 we read "...**God is love**." Praise God! God's love endures because it is an everlasting love!

Jeremiah 31:3

"The Lord appeared to us in the past, saying: '**I have loved you with an everlasting love**; I have drawn you with loving kindness.' "

~~~~~~

Isaiah 43:1-4
"But now, this is what the LORD says--
he who created you, O Jacob,
he who formed you, O Israel:

'Fear not, for I have redeemed you;
I have summoned you by name; you are mine.
**When you pass through the waters,
I will be with you**; and when you pass through the rivers,
they will not sweep over you.

When you walk through the fire, you will not be burned;
the flames will not set you ablaze.
For I am the LORD, your God,
the Holy One of Israel, your Savior;
I give Egypt for your ransom,
Cush and Seba in your stead.
Since **you are precious and honored in my sight**,
and because **I love you**...' "

2. God is caring

You may not care how many hairs you have on your head, but God does! He knows the intricacies of our lives, as Jesus said in Matthew 10:30 **"And even the very hairs of your head are all numbered."**

Matthew 10:29-31
"Are not two sparrows sold for a penny? Yet not one of them will fall to the ground apart from the will of your Father.
And even the very hairs of your head are all numbered. So don't be afraid; **you are worth more than many sparrows."**

Psalm 139:13

"For you created my inmost being; you knit me together in my mother's womb."

In Luke 18:15-16 people were bringing babies to Jesus to have Him touch them. Jesus called the children to Him and said, "Let the little children come to me, and do not hinder them, for the kingdom of God belongs to such as these."

Then Jesus took the children in His arms and blessed them!

3. God is holy

God does not sin. He does not lie. He is incapable of this because He is holy. In John 1:5 we read, **"God is light; in him there is no darkness at all."**

Deuteronomy 32:4
"He is the Rock, **his works are perfect,** and all his ways are just. A faithful **God who does no wrong**, upright and just is he."

+

An angel appeared to Mary to announce she will give birth to Jesus, the holy Son of God.

Luke 1:35
"The angel answered, 'The Holy Spirit will come upon you, and the power of the Most High will overshadow you. **So the holy one to be born will be called the Son of God.** ' "

Jesus tells His disciples in Matthew 5:48:
"Be perfect, therefore, as **your heavenly Father is perfect.**"

4. God is changeless

Do you feel abandoned, mistreated, betrayed? Look up to the heavens! **God loves you with His perfect, pure love!** He will never leave you or forsake you. He is your forever Friend whose love for you does not change. Jesus loves you today with the same intensity of love as when He walked this earth. His love continues on and on, and one day we will see Him face to face in glory with His holy angels!

Hebrews 13:8
"Jesus Christ is the same yesterday and today and forever."

———————————————————————————

I know that my Redeemer lives *

I know that my Redeemer lives
What comfort this sweet sentence gives
He lives, He lives, who once was dead
He lives my ever-living head.

He lives all glory to His name
He lives my Jesus still the same
Oh, the sweet joy this sentence gives
I know that my Redeemer lives!

*The Lutheran Hymnal #200 I Know that My Redeemer Lives

Malachi 3:6
"I the LORD do not change."

___

James 1:17
"Every good and perfect gift is from above, coming down from the Father of the heavenly lights, **who does not change** like shifting shadows."

___

Hebrews 13:5
"...**God has said, 'Never will I leave you; never will I forsake you.' "**

___

Psalm 117:1.2
"Praise the LORD, all you nations;
extol him, all you peoples.
For great is his love toward us,
and **the faithfulness of the LORD endures forever.**
Praise the LORD."

+

___
64

Psalm 136:1, 23-26
"Give thanks to the LORD, for he is good.
His love endures forever.
...to the One who remembered us in our low estate
His love endures forever.
and freed us from our enemies,
His love endures forever.
and who gives food to every creature.
His love endures forever.
Give thanks to the God of heaven.
His love endures forever."

We can count on God's changeless and enduring love. Our loving Lord walks with us right now and right through eternity! His love endures forever! *

* Check http://www.biblegateway.com for more than 50 Bible references for keywords "love endures forever".

Praise God! God is loving and sympathetic, caring, holy, and changeless.

Chapter 7 Jesus: the greatest love of all time

The amazing love of Jesus!

When we look at Jesus' ministry on earth, we can truly see the great love He showed in healing people of diseases and setting people free from evil spirits. The highest expression of His love was when he willingly laid down His life to redeem the world.

Could any of us willingly take the punishment that someone else deserved? Could any of us willingly trade places with a guilty man sentenced to die on death row?... Probably not. But Jesus showed His great love in sacrificing Himself for **our** sins.

I John 4:10
"This is love: not that we loved God, but that he loved us and sent his Son as an atoning sacrifice for our sins."

+

John 15:13
"Greater love has no one than this, that he lay down his life for his friends."

+

Romans 8:32
"He who did not spare His own Son, but gave him up for us all-- how will he not also, along with him, graciously give us all things?"

Jesus suffered pain for us

Because we sin, we deserve death and eternal punishment in hell. It is with sorrow and sadness that we view Jesus nailed to a cross for our sins. Jesus, the sinless Son of God, took our place on the cross. Yet, through the severity of His suffering, we sinful people have peace with God. When Jesus said, "It is finished," the debt which we owed, the punishment for **our** sin, was paid.

Mark 15:24
"And they crucified him."

+

Isaiah 53:5
"But he was pierced for our transgressions, he was crushed for our iniquities; the punishment that brought us peace was upon him, and by his wounds we are healed."

+

When Jesus died on the cross, He took the punishment we deserved for **our** sins. Now we can have the free gift of eternal life in heaven because of God's mercy and grace.

In Peter's Pentecost sermon in Acts 2:23,36, Peter tells the crowd of people gathered:
"...and you, with the help of wicked men, put him to death by nailing him to the cross...Therefore let all Israel be assured of this: God has made this Jesus, whom you crucified, both Lord and Christ."

Philippians 2:5-10

"Your attitude should be the same as that of Christ Jesus:
Who, being in very nature God,
did not consider equality with God something to be grasped,
but made himself nothing,
taking the very nature of a servant,
being made in human likeness.
And being found in appearance as a man,
he humbled himself
and became obedient to death--
even death on a cross!
Therefore God exalted him to the highest place
and gave him the name that is above every name,
that at the name of Jesus every knee should bow,
in heaven and on earth and under the earth..."

Forgiveness through Jesus' blood

When Jesus died in agony on the cross, He was bleeding from the flogging, and the nails in His hands and His feet. A crown of thorns was placed on His innocent head. After He died, a soldier pierced His side and out flowed blood and water (John 20). We are redeemed with the precious blood of Jesus shed for us for the forgiveness of sins.

+

Ephesians 1:7
"In him we have redemption through his blood, the forgiveness of sins..."

+

Colossians 1:19-20
"For God was pleased to have all his fullness dwell in him, and through him to reconcile to himself all things, whether things on earth or things in heaven, by **making peace through his blood, shed on the cross."**

69

Peace through Jesus' resurrection from the dead

On the third day, after Jesus died, He came alive again as He promised He would in John 2:18-22. " (... I will raise it again in three days..." John 2:19). Jesus appeared to his disciples hiding in the upper room, but Thomas, the disciple, was not with the other disciples.

John 20:25-28

"So the other disciples told him, 'We have seen the Lord!'
But he said to them, '**Unless I see the nail marks in his hands and put my finger where the nails were, and put my hand into his side, I will not believe it.**'
A week later his disciples were in the house again, and Thomas was with them. Though the doors were locked, **Jesus came and stood among them and said, 'Peace be with you!' Then he said to Thomas, 'Put your finger here; see my hands. Reach out your hand and put it into my side. Stop doubting and believe.**'
Thomas said to him, 'My Lord and my God!' "

How wonderful it must have been to see Jesus after His resurrection! When Jesus appeared to the disciples on the shores of Lake Galilee and cooked them breakfast, what wonderful fellowship with the Lord, that must have been! When we attend Holy Communion we get a glimpse of what it would be like to be with Jesus in heaven, to attend the heavenly banquet and feel His comfort and peace.

ᏚᏚ

The love of Jesus transformed Esther's life

You can watch a recent video about a desperate woman named Esther on the website on page 70...* Esther was married to a physically and verbally abusive husband who **locked her in a closet** for days at a time. While Esther had done nothing to provoke him, she began to lose more and more of her self-esteem. Esther began to have suicidal thoughts as she walked along the bridge over a busy highway. She had never shared her story with anyone and she thought that jumping was the only way to escape the abusive relationship...

But just as she was going to end her life, her brother drove by and asked her to get into the car. Esther poured out her heart to him and told him everything!

Her brother shared the message of Jesus' great love for her and asked her, "Do you want Jesus in your life?"

Right there in the car, at that moment, Esther accepted Jesus as her personal Savior. After that, she left her abusive husband and began attending church. **She praises Jesus for how He cleansed her life from fears and memories of abuse.**

Esther said, **"No matter what we have gone through, God gives us a new mind and a fresh start. And nothing can compare to that!"**

* http://www.godvone.com/Amazing-Story-of-a-Suicidal-Woman Finding Jesus-164.html

The song "You Raise Me Up" by Josh Groban describes how God lifts us up from a lowly state to stand on mountaintops.
http://www.azlyrics.com/lyrics/joshgroban/youralsemeup.html

Prayer of repentance

+ + + + + + + + + + + + + + +

Dear Jesus:

I am sorry for all of the sins I have done. Thank you for your

perfect love for me. Thank you for dying on a cross for me to

pay the penalty for my sins. Thank you for coming alive on the

third day. Please forgive my sins and walk with me all my days.

Amen

+

Chapter 8 When the house came down

One of the saddest events of my life is when the old farmhouse came down. The old gray homestead had served four generations. Even though the house was old and weatherworn on the outside, to me it was the most beautiful place on earth. It was my dear childhood home. God had richly blessed my childhood with loving parents, three wonderful sisters and a great brother. Among the beautiful memories instilled in my soul are the breath-taking sunsets through the tall evergreen trees, fresh country air, the taste of homemade apple pie, and the fellowship of family devotions.

But when the house came down, tears filled up in my eyes and hundreds of pleasant memories flashed through my mind... My husband reminded me of how I could be thankful that I was raised in a Christian home and that no one could take my pleasant memories from me. More than ever, I rejoiced that my real home is in heaven and that home is eternal!

Jesus the Cornerstone of our foundation

The foundation of the old farmhouse was cracked and crumbling. Yet, all who lived there, by God's grace, had the perfect, firm foundation of God's love with Jesus as the cornerstone.

+

Ephesians 2:19-20
"...you are no longer foreigners and aliens, but fellow citizens with God's people and members of God's household, built on the foundation of the apostles and prophets, with **Christ Jesus himself as the chief cornerstone.**"

+

I Peter 2:6
"For in Scripture it says: 'See, I lay a stone in Zion, a chosen and precious cornerstone, and **the one who trusts in him will never be put to shame.'** "

Jesus is preparing a place for us

Jesus comforts us with these words in John 14:1-3:

"Do not let your hearts be troubled. Trust in God; trust also in me. **In my Father's house are many rooms**; if it were not so, I would have told you. **I am going there to prepare a place for you.** And if I go and prepare a place for you, **I will come back and take you to be with me** that you also may be where I am."

^^

"Heaven is my home"*

I'm but a stranger here
Heaven is my home
Earth is a desert drear
Heaven is my home.
Danger and sorrow stand
Round me on every hand.
Heaven is my Father land
Heaven is my home.

* The Lutheran Hymnal #660

God's Word stands forever

When my dad died in 1992 at the age of 88, and my mom died in 2004 at the age of 90, and when my brother died in 2006 at the age of 52, I attended the same church in my hometown for the funerals. In 2006 I paused to stare at the old brick building, its reddish brown bricks still sturdy and standing straight as the day it was built. After nearly 100 years, it had stood the test of time. Meanwhile, many people in my hometown had died, some young, some old, but the building still stood strong and tall.

God's Word is like that church building, strong and sure. God's Word endures from generation to generation. It endures forever.

I Peter 1:24, 25
"...the word of the Lord stands forever."
+

Matthew 24:35

"Heaven and earth will pass away, but my words will never pass away."

Heaven...the perfect place

When we get to heaven, there will be no more suffering, no more pain, no more dying, and no more crying. The ultimate joy is that we will be with God! Only perfect peace and joy forever!

+

Revelations 21:3-4

"And I heard a loud voice from the throne saying, 'Now the dwelling of God is with men, and he will live with them. They will be his people, and God himself will be with them and be their God. **He will wipe every tear from their eyes. There will be no more death or mourning or crying or pain**, for the old order of things has passed away."

As we wait

What does the future hold? We don't really know. But we know Who holds the future. It is our holy God who cares for us and has unfailing love for us.

In John 14:27 Jesus gives us His peace:

"Peace I leave with you; my peace I give you. I do not give to you as the world gives. Do not let your hearts be troubled and do not be afraid."

Made in the USA
Monee, IL
04 May 2023